ALADDIN PAPERBACKS
An imprint of Simon & Schuster Children's Publishing Division
1230 Avenue of the Americas
New York, New York 10020

Also available in a hardcover edition from
Simon & Schuster Books for Young Readers
Manufactured in the United States of America.

10 9 8 7 6 5 4 3

ISBN: 0-671-73276-5

Daddies at Work

by Eve Merriam • Illustrated by Eugenie Fernandes

Aladdin Paperbacks

Daddies lift you up and swing you around.

Daddies tickle you
with their beards.

Daddies sing silly songs.

Daddies make spaghetti messes.

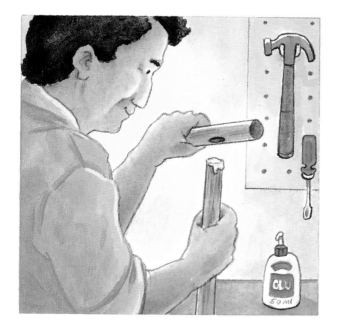

Daddies fix toys that are broken.

Daddies read stories and bring glasses of water.

What other things do daddies do?

All kinds of daddies at all kinds of jobs.

Bus driver daddies.

Carpenter daddies.

Daddies who are doctors.

Daddies who are nurses.

Daddies on fire trucks.

Daddies in parades.

Daddies in tree tops.

Daddies digging holes.

Daddies in the clouds.

Tailor daddies and sailor daddies.

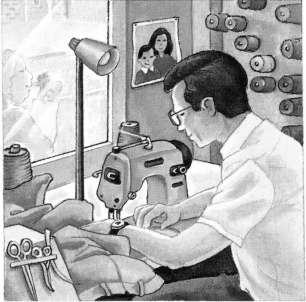

Daddies on horseback.

Hair cutting daddies.

Computer daddies.

Lawyer daddies with egg salad sandwiches in their briefcases.

Laundromat daddies.

Waiter daddies.

Painter daddies.

Umpire daddies.

Daddies working in hotels

and stores and zoos.

Fat daddies,
thin daddies.

Short, tall,
in between
daddies.

Daddies with mustaches

and daddies who are bald . . .

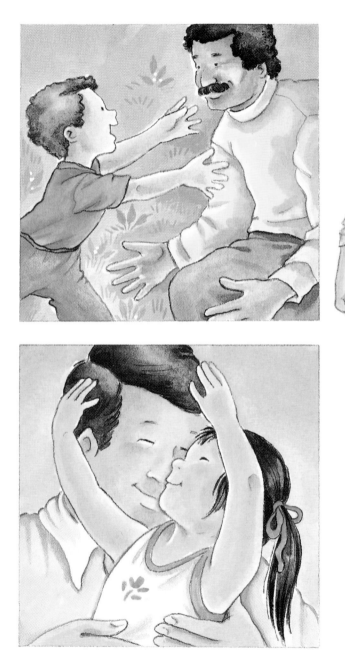

and all daddies everywhere

loving the most of all to be your very own daddy,
and coming home to YOU!

$3.25 U.S.
$4.50 CAN

PQT804230

80998

0 76714 00325 5

ISBN 0-689-80998-0

ALADDIN PAPERBACKS
Simon & Schuster
Ages 3–6
PRINTED IN USA